TRUTH FACTS

TRUTH FACTS

THE TRUTHIEST TRUTHS AND FACTIEST FACTS OF EVERYDAY LIFE

WULFF & MORGENTHALER

HARPER PERENNIAL

NEW YORK • LONDON • TORONTO • SYDNEY • NEW DELHI • AUCKLAND

HARPER ● PERENNIAL

HarperCollins books may be purchased for educational, business, or sales promotional use. For information, please e-mail the Special Markets Department at SPsales@harpercollins.com.

FIRST EDITION

Designed by Leydiana Rodriguez

Library of Congress Cataloging-in-Publication Data has been applied for.

ISBN 978-0-06-248626-4 (pbk.)

16 17 18 19 20 10 9 8 7 6 5 4 3 2 1

INTRODUCTION

The truth is something people like to think they appreciate. In reality, though, the truth is highly unpopular. It's in the same league as warts, the smell of wet dog, or carnies moving into your garage. Our personal experience with the truth is such that whenever we have taken a chance and tried to use it in real life, whether in a relationship or a professional context, it has led to divorce, years of therapy, grounds for firing, kicks in the stomach with pointy boots, and a dude in a bar taking a swing at us with a shovel.

None of this is particularly nice. So we wondered: How can we make the truth something that we can share, without causing people to physically attack us? The answer: Good-looking graphics.

So we started to create infographics, with pleasing colors and nicely done pie charts and diagrams. Into these clean, good-looking graphics, we poured all the facts of life and all the truth that is hard to tell. We called our invention Truth Facts.

Since starting to tell the truth by using only Truth Facts, we have not made a single new enemy and our love lives and professional careers have blossomed, leading to phenomenal success and happiness. Truth Facts show that, at long last, it's possible for mankind to communicate truthfully without it leading to violent outbursts or yearlong grievances. Instead, Truth Facts will lead to world peace and solve most problems. We're telling the truth.

Best,
Wulff & Morgenthaler

TRUTH FACTS

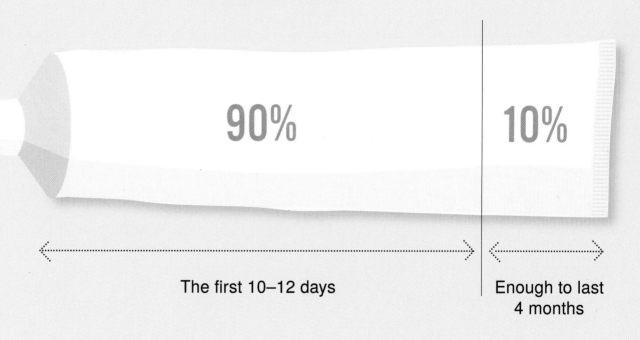

TOOTHPASTE

90%   10%

The first 10–12 days | Enough to last 4 months

CONTENT OF WOMEN'S MAGAZINES

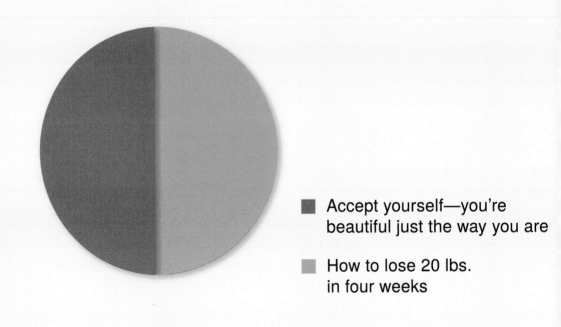

■ Accept yourself—you're
beautiful just the way you are

■ How to lose 20 lbs.
in four weeks

THE McDONALD'S CURVE

I'm lovin' it!

Never again

COMPONENTS OF NACHOS

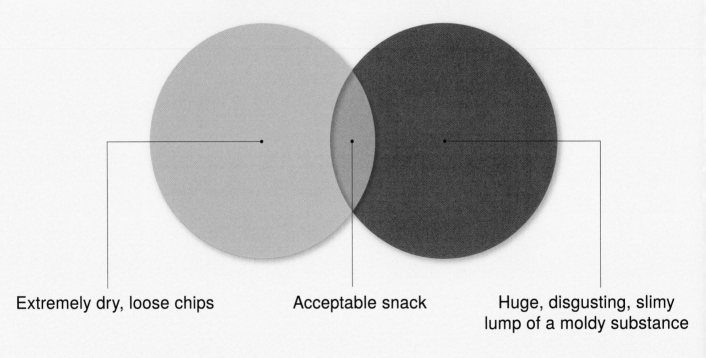

Extremely dry, loose chips　　Acceptable snack　　Huge, disgusting, slimy lump of a moldy substance

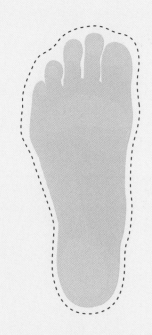

What a foot looks like

What shoe manufacturers
think a foot looks like

5

THE ANATOMY OF BACON

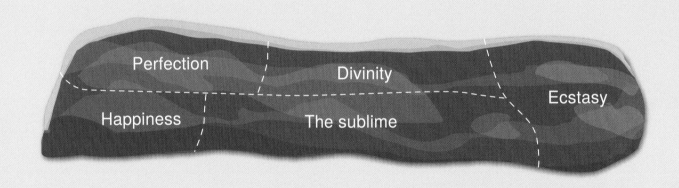

THERE ARE TWO KINDS OF PEOPLE

A Those who get it

B Those who don't get it

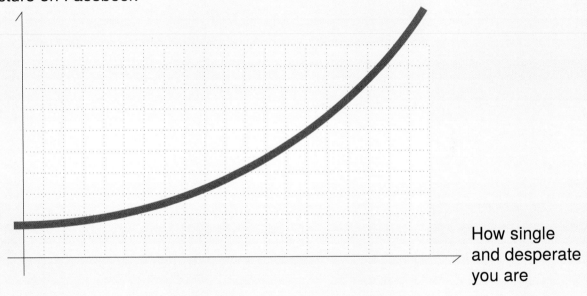

How often you change your profile picture on Facebook

How single and desperate you are

SURVEILLANCE SOCIETY

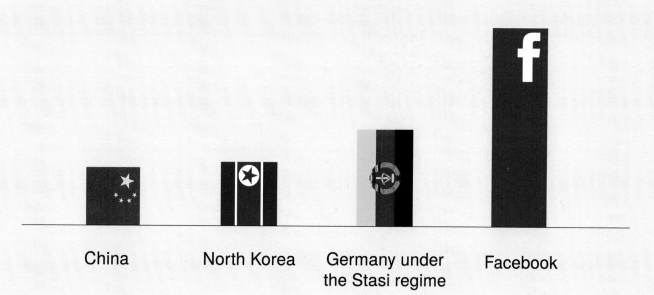

BIRTHDAY GREETINGS ON YOUR FACEBOOK WALL

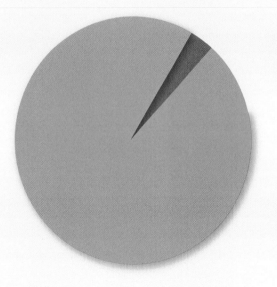

■ Annoying people who only post on your wall because they expect you to write on their wall for their birthday to make them seem popular

■ People who actually hope you have a happy birthday

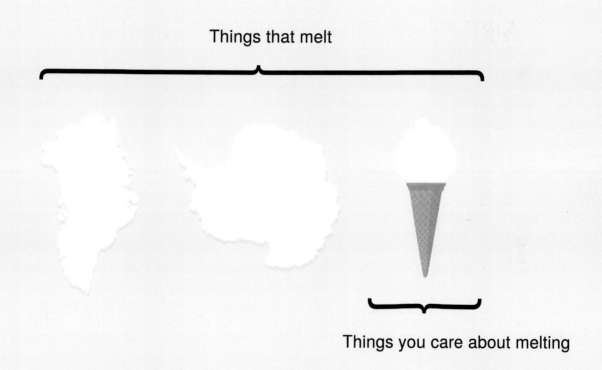

MEN'S CONSUMPTION OF PORNOGRAPHY

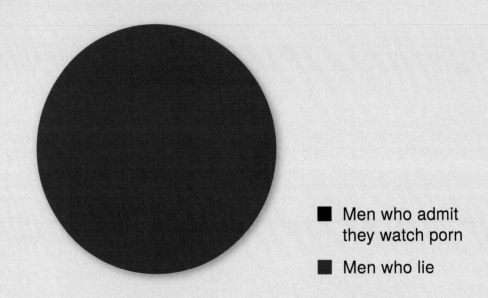

- Men who admit they watch porn
- Men who lie

Restraint   Precision   Creativity   Panic

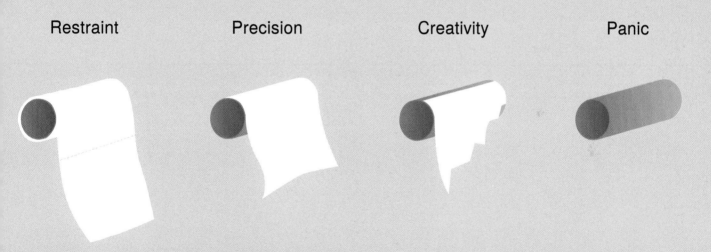

13

FOOD PYRAMID FOR HANGOVERS

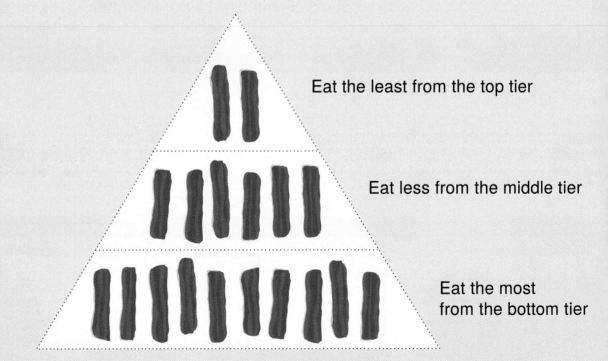

Eat the least from the top tier

Eat less from the middle tier

Eat the most
from the bottom tier

OPENING HOURS OF BANKS

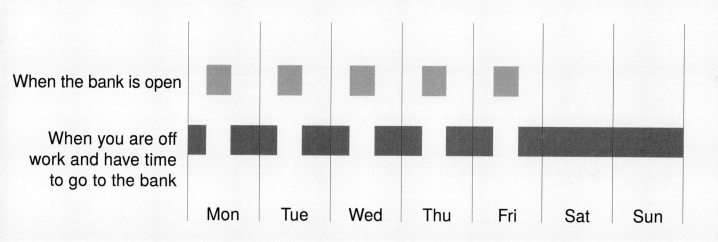

LEVEL OF FINE MOTOR SKILLS

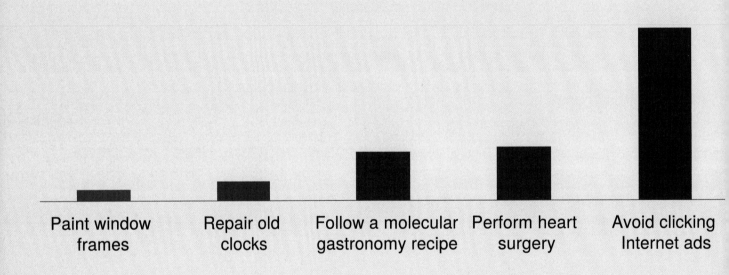

Paint window frames | Repair old clocks | Follow a molecular gastronomy recipe | Perform heart surgery | Avoid clicking Internet ads

STATISTICS SHOW THAT TEEN PREGNANCIES DROP DRASTICALLY AFTER THE AGE OF 20

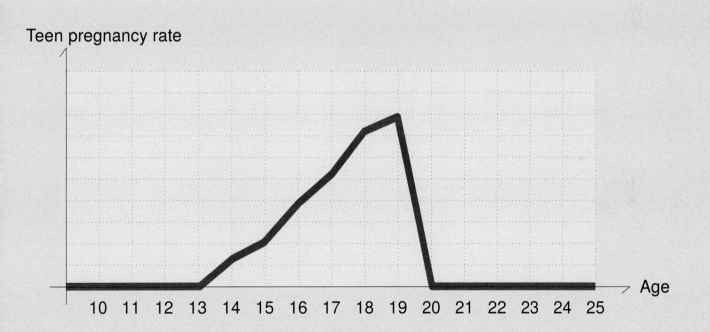

YOUR WHEREABOUTS

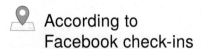 According to
Facebook check-ins

Reality

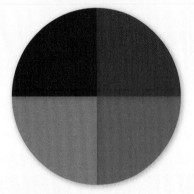

■ At a gourmet restaurant
■ At the airport
■ At an art opening
■ At a VIP event

■ At home in your
dirty underwear
in front of your
computer

WHEN YOU'RE GOING TO THE MOVIES

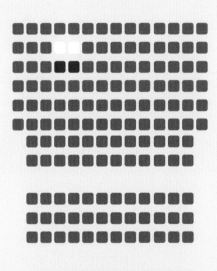

The seats you've carefully selected

Seats with people of average proportion

Seats with supernaturally tall people

19

GUIDE TO TAN LINES

Bicycling vacation

Golf vacation

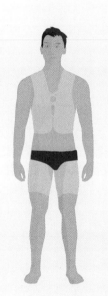

Water sports vacation

Vacation in Seattle

CONSUMPTION OF DENTAL FLOSS

■ Day before dentist appointment

■ Rest of year

GUIDE TO LAUNDRY

Advanced

Easy

SHOOTING ACCURACY AGAINST THE HERO IN AN ACTION MOVIE

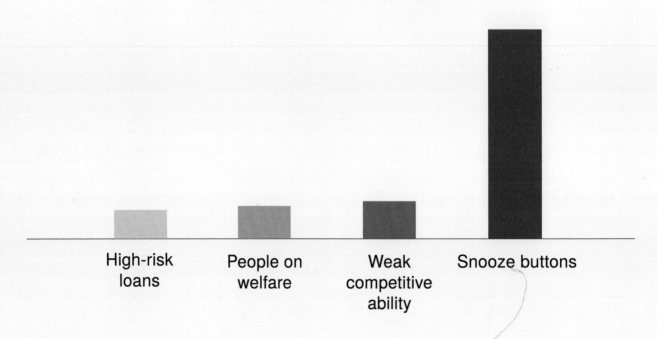

OCCURRENCES OF ACNE

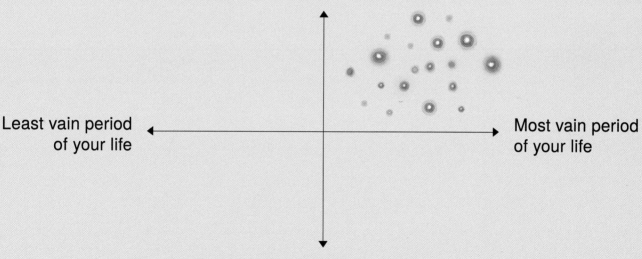

Most visible place on your body

Least vain period of your life

Most vain period of your life

Least visible place on your body

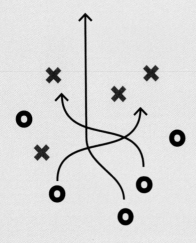

Offensive strategy in the NFL

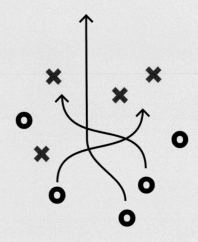

How you avoid pedestrian collisions in Times Square

STUFF PEOPLE SAY AT PARTIES	WHAT THEY MEAN
WUUUH!	I have low self-esteem.
Can my friends stop by?	Is it okay if a gang robs your house?
You wanna grab a cigarette?	Should we talk behind people's backs?
I rarely drink.	I rarely drink less than ten shots.
CHEERS!	Hold me!
I spilled on your sofa.	I peed on your sofa.
Let me just find a song.	I'll take over Spotify for the next five hours.
I need to dance tonight.	I need to have sex with someone tonight.

MOST EFFECTIVE MAKEUP REMOVERS

Skin-care products

Relationships

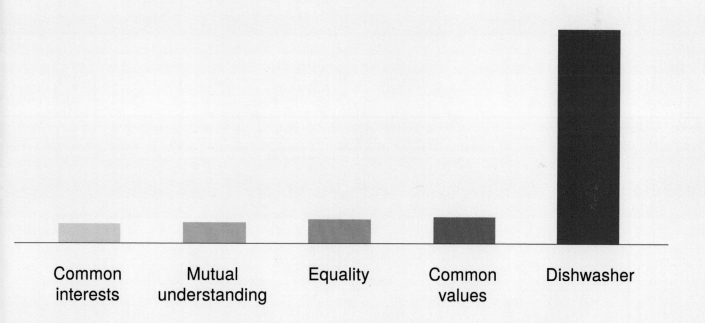

FACTORS THAT PROLONG A RELATIONSHIP

Common interests

Mutual understanding

Equality

Common values

Dishwasher

29

WHAT HELICOPTERS DO IN MOVIES

■ Explode

JOB TITLES: 1950

Farmer

Worker

Businessman

JOB TITLES: NOW

Strategic
Chief
Creative
Principal
Corporate
Senior
Digital

Brand
Innovation
Social Media
Identity
Division
Marketing
Development

Executive
Expert
Officer
Manager
Director
Associate
Guru

WHEN A GIRL GETS CHANGED IN FRONT OF YOU

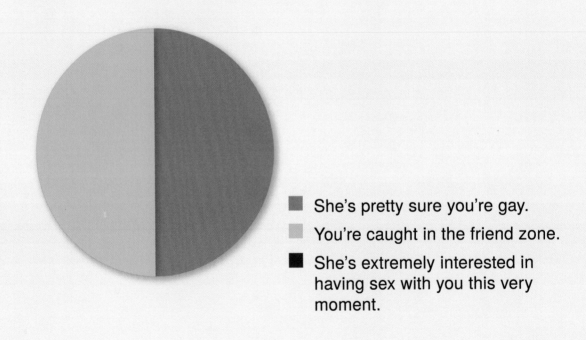

- ■ She's pretty sure you're gay.
- ■ You're caught in the friend zone.
- ■ She's extremely interested in having sex with you this very moment.

USE OF LAUNDRY LABEL

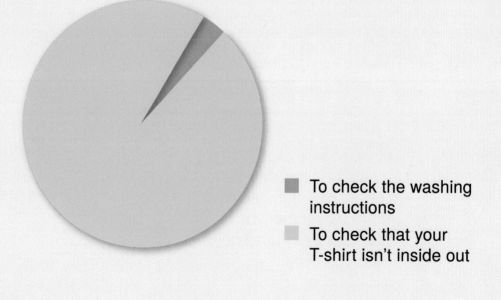

■ To check the washing instructions

■ To check that your T-shirt isn't inside out

WHAT THE VARIOUS FUNCTIONS ON FACEBOOK MEAN

LIKE
I'm too lazy to comment on what you wrote.

FRIEND REQUEST
Hi, I'd like to check out your private photos way too intensely.

CHECK IN
My life is frequently boring. Therefore, it's important to me that everybody is informed that I have now left my house.

POKE
Saw your pictures—now I'd like to have sex as well.

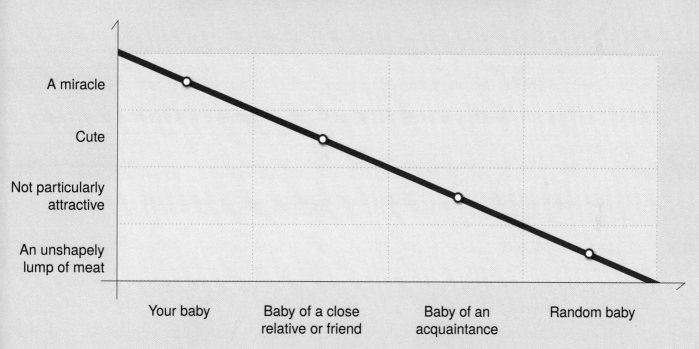

LEVEL OF BABIES' ATTRACTIVENESS

A miracle

Cute

Not particularly
attractive

An unshapely
lump of meat

Your baby

Baby of a close
relative or friend

Baby of an
acquaintance

Random baby

EVOLUTION OF DIGITAL MEDIA

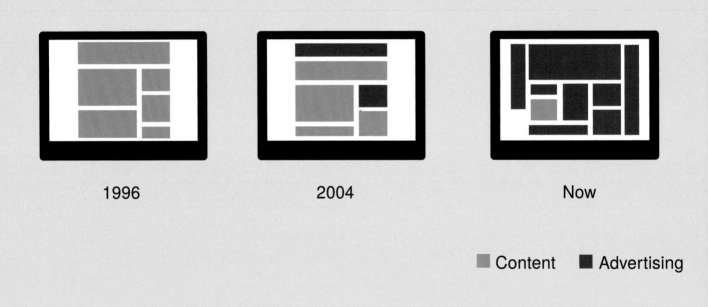

1996   2004   Now

Content   Advertising

GREAT REGRETS OF MANKIND

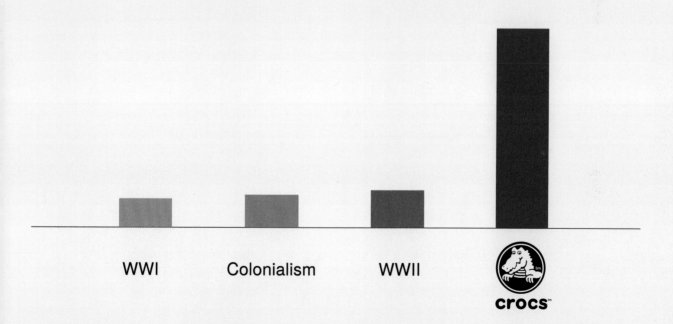

STUFF YOU SAY IN A JOB INTERVIEW

WHAT YOU MEAN

STUFF YOU SAY IN A JOB INTERVIEW	WHAT YOU MEAN
I'm interested in the job.	I'm broke.
I'm a team player.	I let other people do my work.
My biggest weakness is honesty.	My biggest strength is lying.
I went to law school.	I've seen *Boston Legal*.
I have no criminal record.	They never found the bodies.
I love a challenge.	I play Candy Crush during work hours.
The pay isn't important.	I steal office supplies.
I'm always in a good mood.	I'm high when I show up to work.

IMPROVEMENTS TO THE CURRENT CALENDAR WEEK

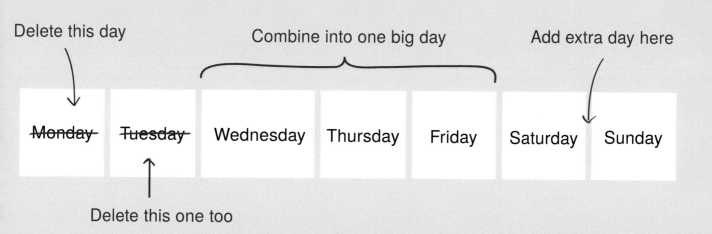

HOW LONG "NEVER" LASTS

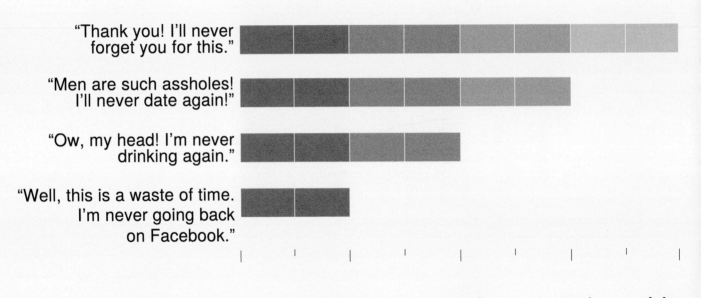

"Thank you! I'll never forget you for this."

"Men are such assholes! I'll never date again!"

"Ow, my head! I'm never drinking again."

"Well, this is a waste of time. I'm never going back on Facebook."

1 hour   1 week   1 month   A few months

Men's sandals

Sandals that look good on men

41

THERE ARE TWO KINDS OF MEN

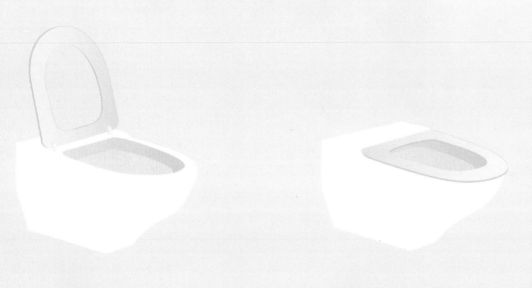

 A Single

B In a long-term relationship

THE EVOLUTION OF LANGUAGE

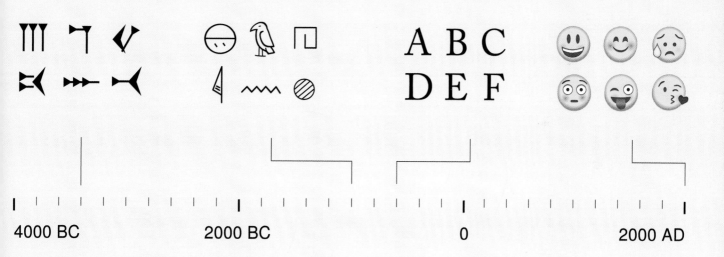

4000 BC   2000 BC   0   2000 AD

YOUR STEREO

MIN   MAX

YOUR NEIGHBOR'S STEREO

MAX   YOUR MAXIMUM x 10

TECHNO

WHAT TRAFFIC LIGHTS MEAN

Regular drivers	Stop	Wait	Go
Cab drivers	Go	Go	Go

45

YOUR WIFI CONNECTION

When you
don't need
the Internet

When you're
checking
Facebook

When you
have to respond
to an e-mail ASAP

When you
need to show somebody
a hilarious YouTube clip

46

ASSIGNMENT OF AIRPLANE SEATS

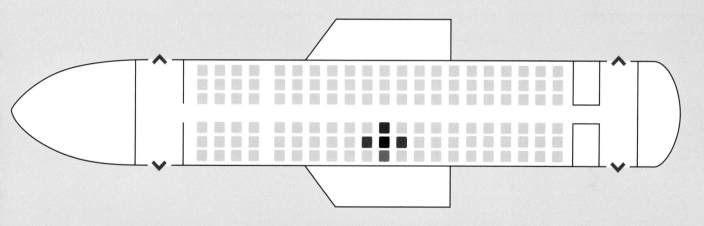

- ■ Here is your seat
- ■ Screaming baby
- ■ Fast-asleep passenger
- ■ Incessantly talkative passenger
- ■ Drunk tourist
- ■ Regular passenger

47

GRILLED STEAK

GRILLED CHICKEN

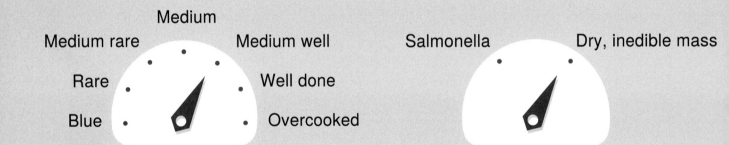

Medium

Medium rare

Medium well

Rare

Well done

Blue

Overcooked

Salmonella

Dry, inedible mass

AT THE DENTIST

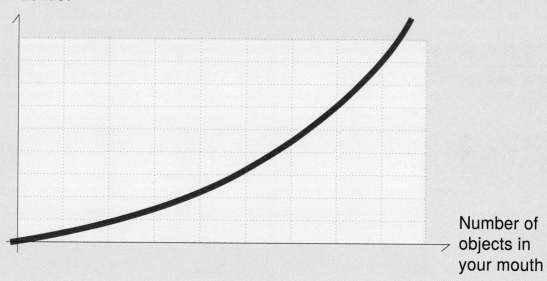

Number of personal questions from your dentist

Number of objects in your mouth

WHAT STORES PROCLAIM	WHAT IT MEANS
SPECIAL OFFER!	Same price as always.
HALF PRICE!	Still double the amount of what it really should cost.
BUY TWO, GET ONE FREE!	Nevermind that you only need one.
NOW ONLY $100, SAVE $50!	Waste $100 on something you don't need.
SAVE UP TO 70%!	Save down to 0%.
CLEARANCE SALE!	We'll close shop when we have your money.
IT'S OUR BIRTHDAY!	Just like it was last month.
FINAL SALE!	Stuff nobody wanted can be yours!

ONLINE DATING

Where people who use
online dating meet

■ Online

Where people who use
online dating say they met

■ During a night out
■ At a concert
■ At the grocery store
■ Through a friend
you've never met
■ Online

51

When you buy it   When you put it in your bag   When you want to eat it

COFFEE BEVERAGES

Black coffee

Coffee with cream and/or sugar

Cappuccino
Single Latte
Double Latte
Triple Latte
Single Espresso
Double Espresso
Gibraltar
Café au Lait
Café con Leche
Americano
Caffè Tobio
Affogato
Mocha
Caffè Corretto

Frappe
Frappuccino
Pocillo
Espressino
Flat White
Caffé Misto
Half-caf
Melange
Ristretto
Skinny Latte
Soy/Almond Latte
Chai Latte
Iced Coffee
French Press
Marocchino

In 1996

Now

THE MOST DANGEROUS FOOD ACCORDING TO DIETARY EXPERTS

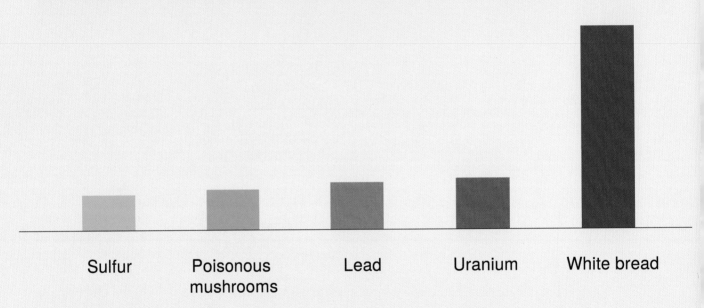

Sulfur | Poisonous mushrooms | Lead | Uranium | White bread

BASIC DANCE STEPS

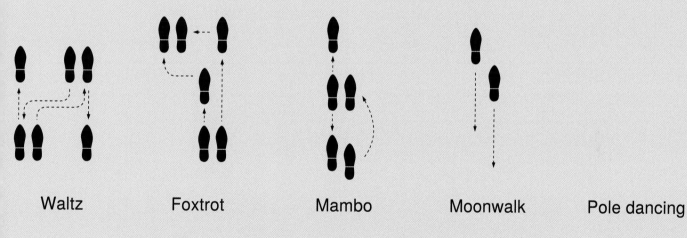

Waltz   Foxtrot   Mambo   Moonwalk   Pole dancing

BLUEPRINT OF IKEA

entrance >
exit <

things you need to buy

THE BIGGEST LIES ON THE INTERNET

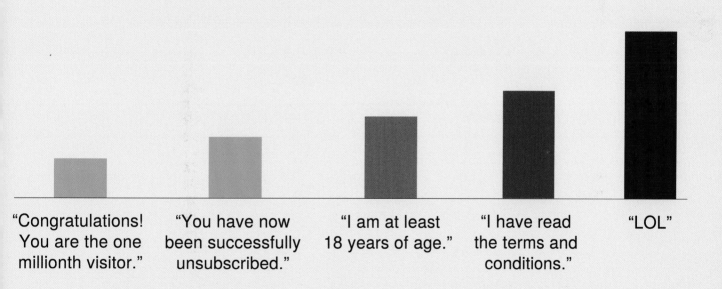

"Congratulations! You are the one millionth visitor."

"You have now been successfully unsubscribed."

"I am at least 18 years of age."

"I have read the terms and conditions."

"LOL"

57

KEYS YOU WISH WORKED IN REAL LIFE

PEDESTRIANS

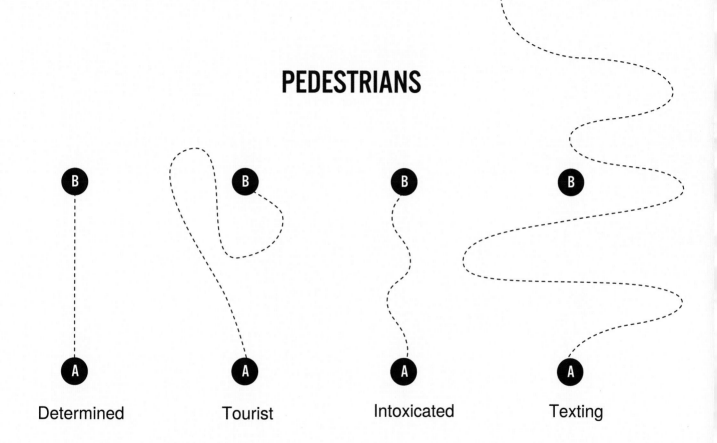

Determined   Tourist   Intoxicated   Texting

WHAT IT MEANS WHEN SOMEONE SAYS YOU LOOK TIRED

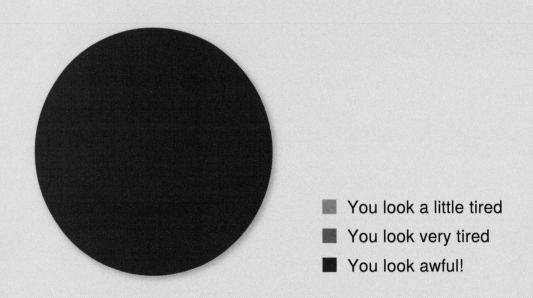

■ You look a little tired
■ You look very tired
■ You look awful!

INFO LISTED ON DATING PROFILES

WHAT IT MEANS

INFO LISTED ON DATING PROFILES	WHAT IT MEANS
I'm a man in my prime.	I'm really old.
I like cozy nights in,	I'm lazy,
but try to keep an active lifestyle.	and should exercise more.
I'm an intelligent man,	I've been bullied quite a bit in my time,
with my feet firmly planted on the ground.	and I lack ambition.
I'm not currently looking for a commitment,	All I want is sex,
but let's see what happens.	so let's meet up and sleep together.

WHAT SMOKE DETECTORS WARN YOU OF

■ Fire hazard
■ Your abilities in a kitchen

HOW PARENTS EVALUATE CHILDREN'S DRAWINGS

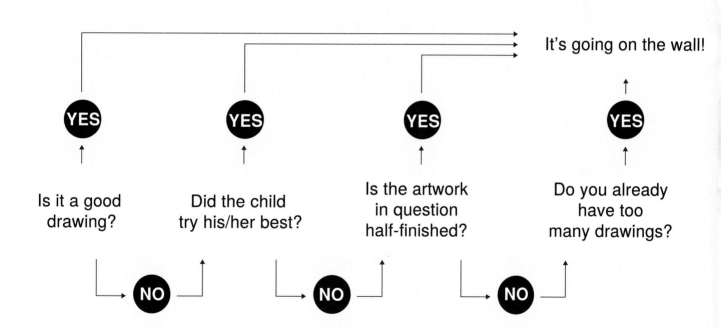

It's going on the wall!

YES — Is it a good drawing?

YES — Did the child try his/her best?

YES — Is the artwork in question half-finished?

YES — Do you already have too many drawings?

NO

NO

NO

63

THE HOLIDAY SEASON IN THE RETAIL INDUSTRY

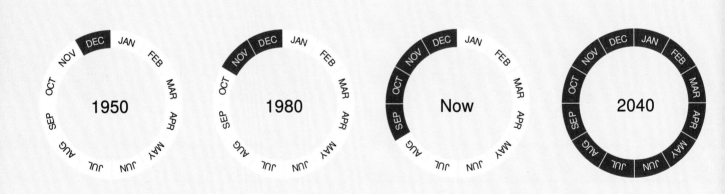

RAPPER NAME GENERATOR

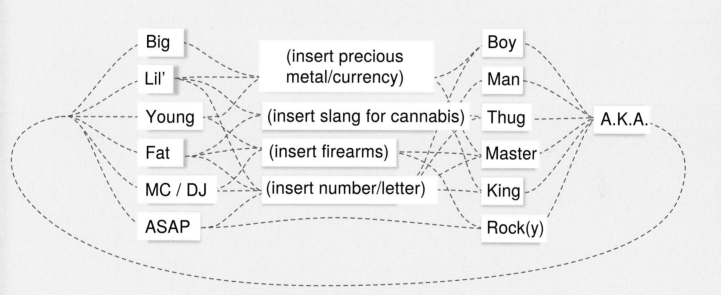

THE WORLD'S MOST FEROCIOUS ANIMALS

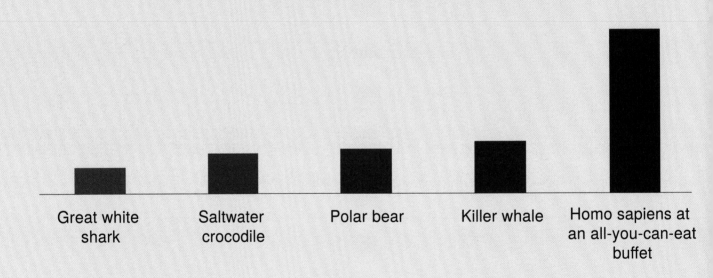

Great white shark | Saltwater crocodile | Polar bear | Killer whale | Homo sapiens at an all-you-can-eat buffet

WASHING SOCKS

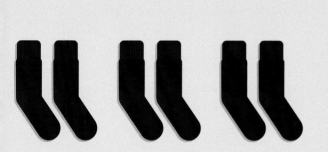

Input

Output

LEVEL OF PRIVACY IN RELATIONSHIPS

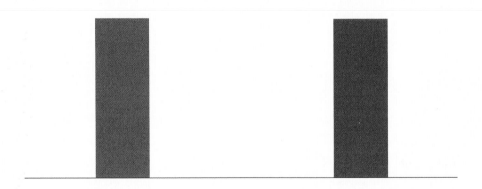

Extremely intimate things that only your girlfriend knows about you

Extremely intimate things that your girlfriend's girlfriends know about you

RELIGIOUS EXTREMISM

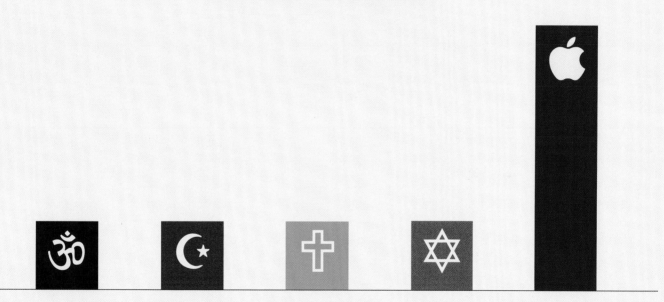

CELL PHONES THEN & NOW

Battery life	3-4 days	3-4 hours
Impact limit	Third floor (asphalt)	2 feet (hardwood floors)
Impact protection	Built-in	Needs add-ons
Software updates	Unnecessary	Approx. once a week
Life span	Still going	Max. 1–2 years
Typing speed	9 characters per second	Damn you, autocorrect!

HOLLYWOOD MOVIES

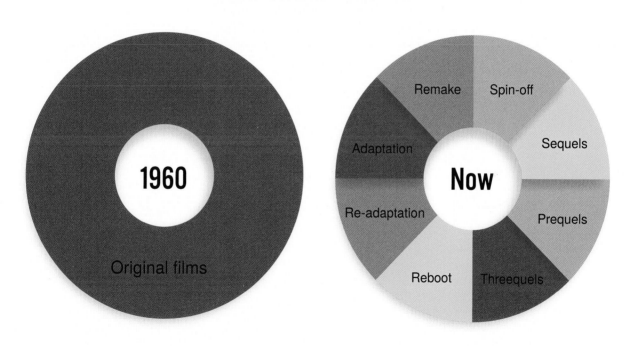

CHRISTMAS CAROLS

Silent night, holy night
All is calm, all is bright
Round yon Virgin Mother and Child
Holy Infant so tender and mild
Sleep in heavenly peace
Sleep in heavenly peace

Silent night, holy night!
Shepherds quake at the sight
Glories stream from heaven afar
Heavenly hosts sing Alleluia!
Christ, the Savior is born
Christ, the Savior is born ...

Original version

Your version

Silent night, holy night
Mmmmmmmmmm
Mmmmmmmmmmmm
Mmmmmmmmmmm
Mmmmmmmmmm
Mmmmmmmmmm

Mmmmmmmmm
Mmmmmmmmmmm
Mmmmmmmmmmmm
Mmmmmmmmmmm
Mmmmmmmmmm
Mmmmmmmmmm

E-MAIL SIGNATURES	WHAT IT MEANS
With love	I'm trying to erode the meaning of the word love.
Sent from my iPhone	I'm not sure where to change this in my settings.
♥.¸¸.•´¯`Be yourself, everyone else is already taken .¸¸.•´¯`♥	Hopefully I'm an insecure 14-year-old girl.
J	I use a ridiculous e-mail client (Outlook). This is a smiley.
Save the forest—don't print	Makes you feel bad, makes me feel like a saint.
E-mail: yourname@gmail.com	I love redundant info.
Connect with me here:	I'm a social media guru. And I'm a fool.

THE COURSE OF A RELATIONSHIP

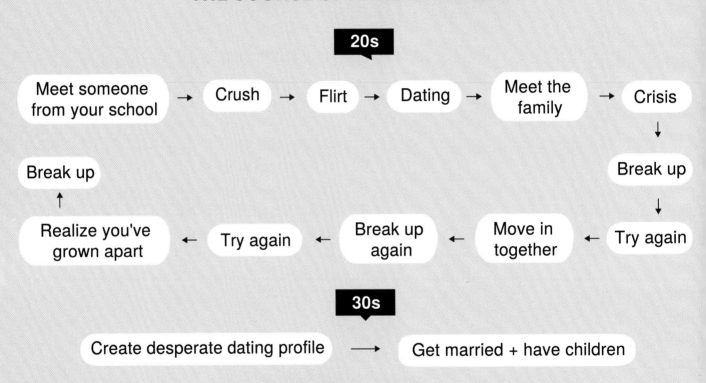

SELF-DIAGNOSIS WITH WEBMD.COM

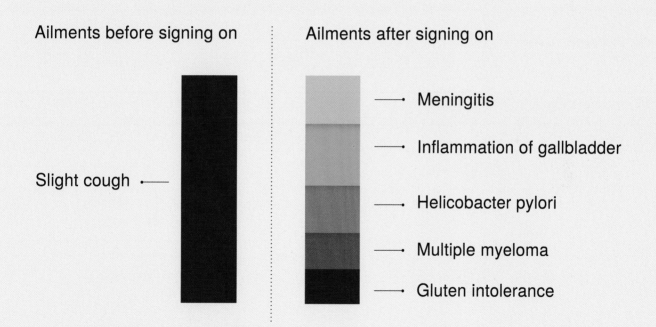

Ailments before signing on

Ailments after signing on

Slight cough

Meningitis

Inflammation of gallbladder

Helicobacter pylori

Multiple myeloma

Gluten intolerance

WHAT YOU GET WHEN YOU CALL CUSTOMER SERVICE

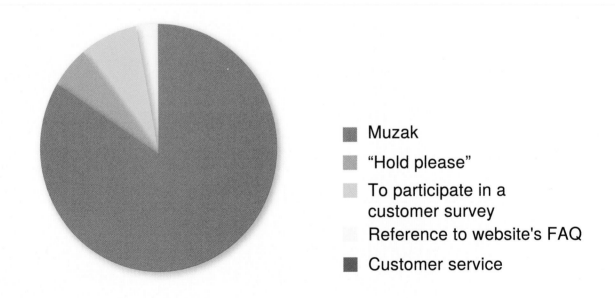

- Muzak
- "Hold please"
- To participate in a customer survey
- Reference to website's FAQ
- Customer service

URGE TO PEE WHILE AT THE MOVIES

BREAKING NEWS IN THE MEDIA LANDSCAPE

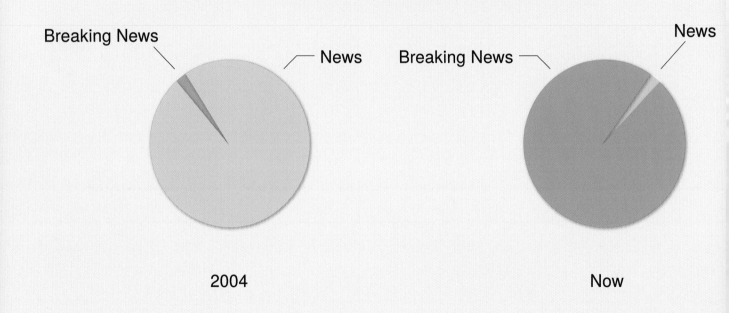

Breaking News

News

2004

Breaking News

News

Now

Souvenirs you think are decorative and necessary to bring back to your home country.

Souvenirs you think are decorative and necessary when back home.

WHAT ANNOYS YOU THE MOST

Social injustice   Religious extremism   Java updates

STUFF YOUR PARENTS SAY	WHAT THEY MEAN
Back when I was a kid ...	My memory is bad, so I'm just making up stuff.
We'll see.	Let's wait until you've forgotten all about it.
Ask your dad.	I'm tired.
Money doesn't grow on trees.	I'm buying a new handbag for myself.
Because I said so!	Your argument is valid, but I'm older!
You're too young to understand.	I have difficulty justifying this.
You'll understand when you're older.	I still don't understand this.

THE SUPERHERO CONSENSUS

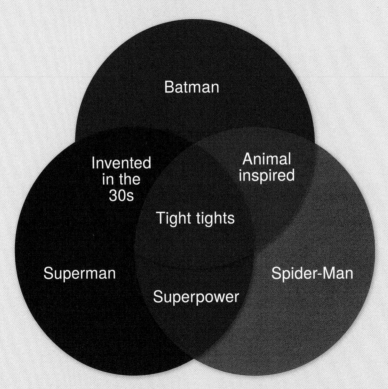

ENJOYING A MOMENT

Previously

Now

83

HOW TO CONTRIBUTE TO A BETTER WORLD

What you could do

✓ Donate money

✓ Organize food drives in your area

✓ Work actively for human rights

✓ Volunteer for Doctors Without Borders

✓ Civic engagement

What you do

 Like and share updates on charities

DANGER SIGNALS

Danger signals you
should care about.

Danger signals you
actually care about.

CANDY STORE WEIGH-INS

Expectation

Reality

KNOW YOUR MUSHROOMS

Edible

Lethally poisonous

ACTIVITIES AFTER HAVING CHILDREN

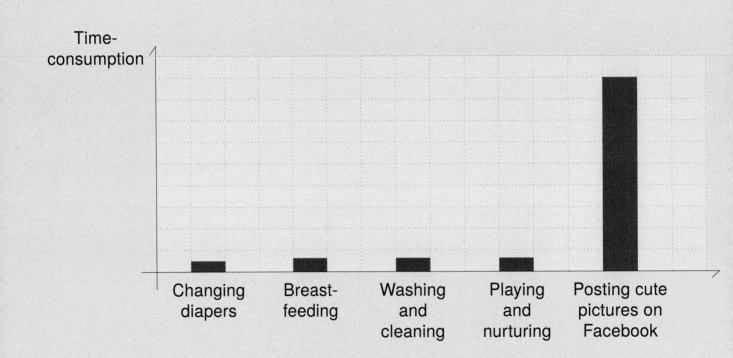

Time-consumption

Changing diapers | Breast-feeding | Washing and cleaning | Playing and nurturing | Posting cute pictures on Facebook

EARPHONES

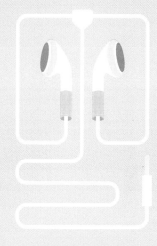

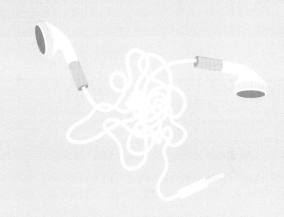

At purchase

After two seconds in your pocket

OUTFIT CRISIS

THE ATTRACTION PARADOX

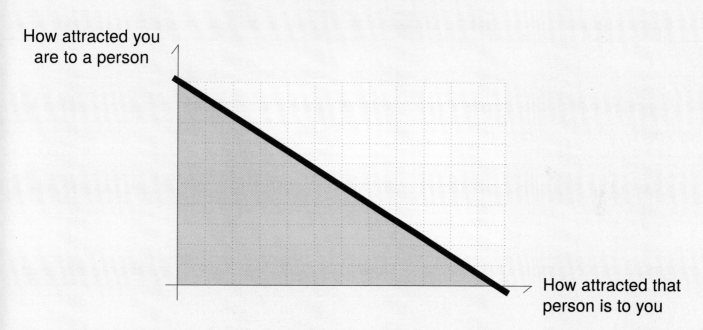

How attracted you
are to a person

How attracted that
person is to you

FASHION

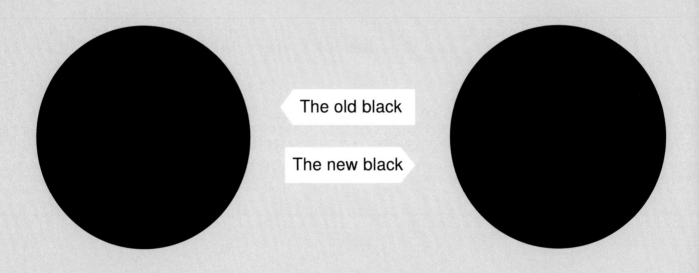

SCHEDULE FOR YOUR WEEKEND

Pre-party

Party

After-party

Drunch

"I HEAR WHAT YOU'RE SAYING, BUT ..."

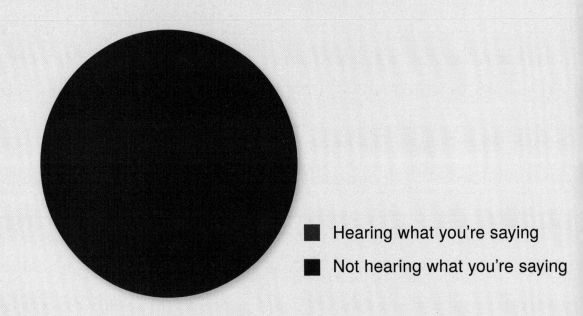

■ Hearing what you're saying

■ Not hearing what you're saying

WHAT GIRLFRIENDS TELL EACH OTHER	WHAT THEY REALLY MEAN
That dress looks good on you.	I wouldn't wear that if I were you.
You were too good for him.	He was out of your league.
Don't worry, it was probably his sister.	He's definitely cheating on you.
I had two cookies earlier, you can have the last one.	Watching you eat that will make me feel better about myself.
I've had sex with five people.	I've had sex with 15 people.
You need a man that can handle you.	You're obnoxious and a bit of a handful.
Your secret is safe with me.	This is great gossip, can't wait to tell everyone.

YOUR REMOTE CONTROL

Available buttons

Buttons you use

YOUR SUBURBAN NEIGHBORHOOD

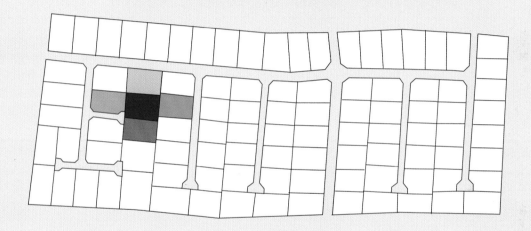

■ You
live here

■ Constantly
mows the lawn

■ Pit bull
enthusiasts

■ Garage
rock band

■ Creepy
naked dude

□ Regular people

WHAT YOUR ZODIAC SIGN SAYS ABOUT YOU

You are a superstitious fool.

SIT-UPS

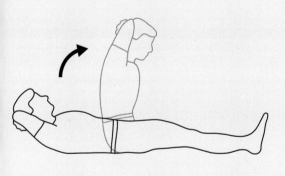

The correct version

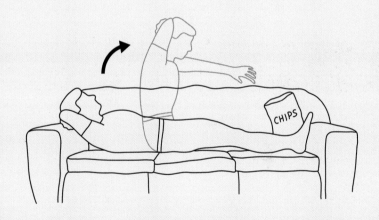

Your version

MUST-HAVES FOR SHOWERING

WHERE THE REST OF THE WORLD GETS ITS KNOWLEDGE OF THE UNITED STATES FROM

Geography class   Traveling   Conversations with Americans   Wikipedia   The Kardashians

WHAT YOUR PET INDICATES

You're incapable of communicating with humans.

You love the smell of urine.

You like watching animals do mindless tasks.

You enjoy watching animals have way more sex than you do.

You live alone.

STUFF POLITICIANS SAY

It's time for reforms!

We must protect our core values ...

Going forward ...

I'm fighting for a better future for us all ...

We need safety in these challenging times ...

I promise to ...

It's time to put this behind us and focus on the issues at hand ...

WHAT THEY MEAN

It's time for cutbacks!

Let's not try something new!

Ignore my previous mistakes!

I'm fighting for a salary bump for myself ...

I owe a favor to these guys in the arms industry ...

Wouldn't it be great if ...

I'm sorry!

YOUR MAC CHARGER

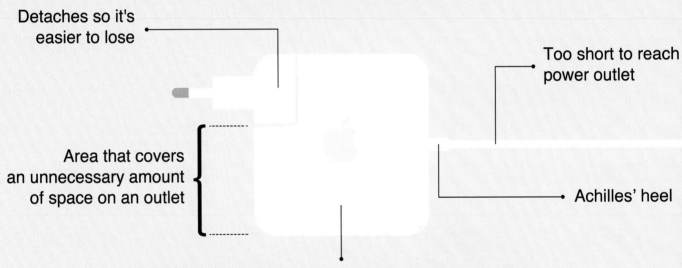

Detaches so it's easier to lose

Too short to reach power outlet

Area that covers an unnecessary amount of space on an outlet

Achilles' heel

Substantial weight so it can barely hang in an outlet

HOW YOU LEAVE A ROLL OF TAPE

Thoughtful person

Jackass

A DAY OF WORK

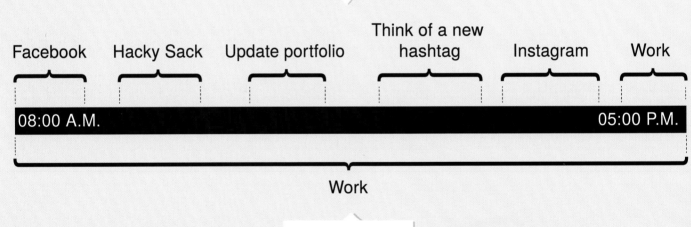

WHAT YOUR TEETH SAY ABOUT YOU

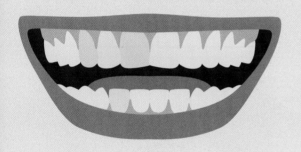

You have bad habits

You have bad friends

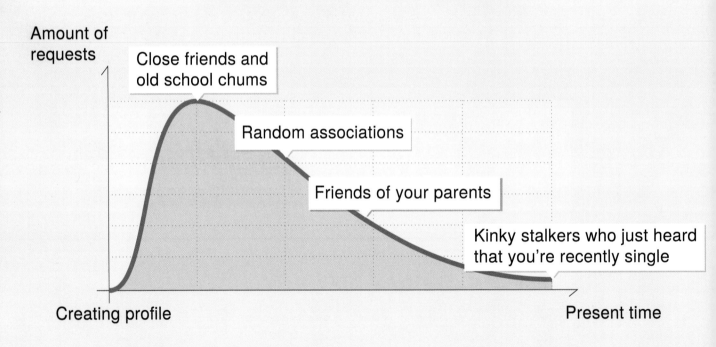

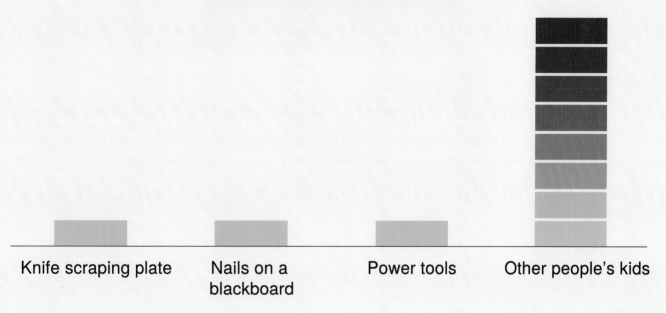

MOST ANNOYING SOUNDS

Knife scraping plate   Nails on a blackboard   Power tools   Other people's kids

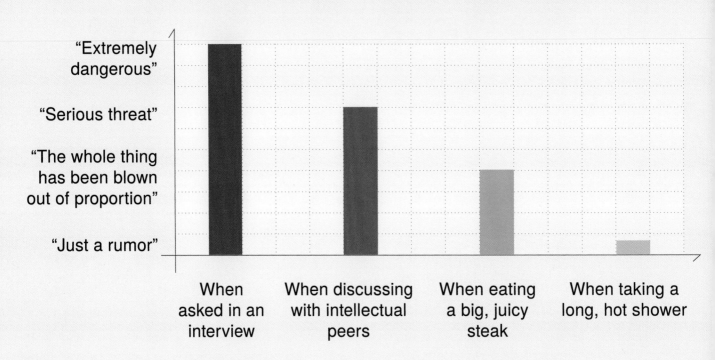

YOUR PERCEPTION OF GLOBAL WARMING

"Extremely dangerous"

"Serious threat"

"The whole thing has been blown out of proportion"

"Just a rumor"

When asked in an interview

When discussing with intellectual peers

When eating a big, juicy steak

When taking a long, hot shower

WHAT YOU GET FROM A DATE ON tinder

Expectation

Reality

GUIDE TO UNDERSTANDING YOUR TAX FORMS

PHOTOGRAPHY THEN AND NOW

24	Pictures you take	4000
24	Pictures you develop	0
24	Pictures you look at	0

WHO SPIES ON YOU VIA FACEBOOK

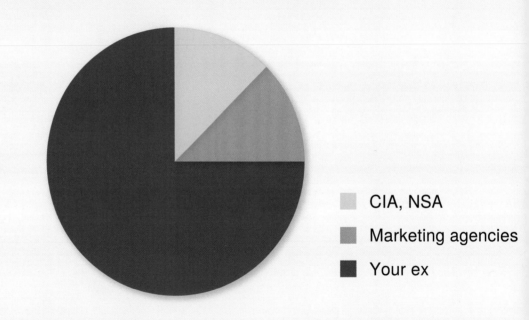

- CIA, NSA
- Marketing agencies
- Your ex

QUALITY TIME WITH KIDS

Before

Now

STUFF TEACHERS SAY	WHAT THEY MEAN
He's a quiet boy.	I suspect he'll turn into a homicidal maniac.
Likes working on his own	Your kid is pretty unpopular.
Full of energy	He definitely has ADHD!
Independent kid	Obnoxious kid
She should be held back a grade.	Get your brat away from me!
She really should skip a grade.	Get your brat away from me!
Your kid is an excellent student.	I heard you were a single mom. Fancy a date?
Do you help out with homework?	Stop it, you're dumber than your kid!

YOUR UPSTAIRS NEIGHBOR'S SCHEDULE

06 A.M.	Loud wake-up music
07 A.M.	Recreational drilling
08 A.M.	Move furniture around
09 A.M.	Check volume levels for the TV
03 P.M.	Practice clog dancing
07 P.M.	Loud fight
09 P.M.	Loud make-up sex
11 P.M.	PARTYYYY!!

CLEAREST SIGN OF AGING

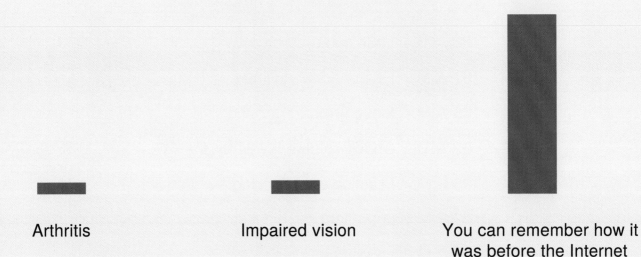

Arthritis

Impaired vision

You can remember how it
was before the Internet

THE DESIGN OF AN IRON

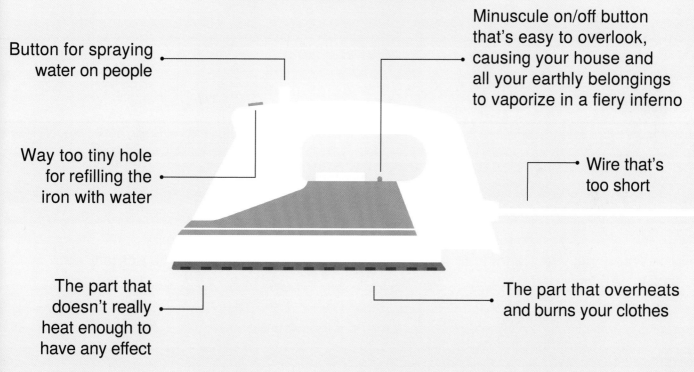

Button for spraying
water on people

Minuscule on/off button
that's easy to overlook,
causing your house and
all your earthly belongings
to vaporize in a fiery inferno

Way too tiny hole
for refilling the
iron with water

Wire that's
too short

The part that
doesn't really
heat enough to
have any effect

The part that overheats
and burns your clothes

WATCHING NETFLIX

When you are planning to stop

When you actually stop

120

"IT'S NOT YOU, IT'S ME ..."

It is you.

HANDY MANUAL FOR YOUR SELFIE STICK

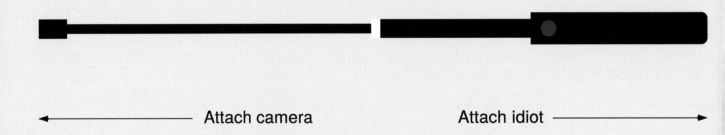

← Attach camera · Attach idiot →

YOUR WORKOUT PLAN

Warm up	Cardio	Strength	Stretching	Upload selfie

YOUR 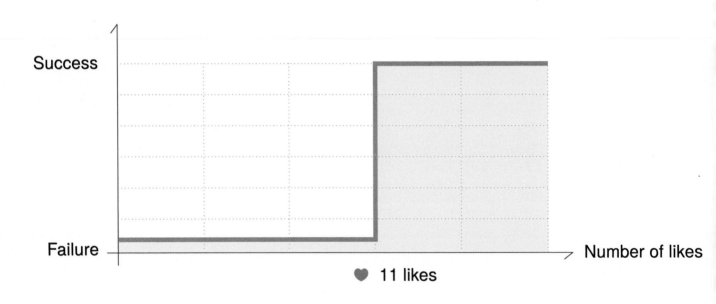 ON INSTAGRAM

Success

Failure ··· Number of likes

🖤 11 likes

THE IRONMAN TYPE

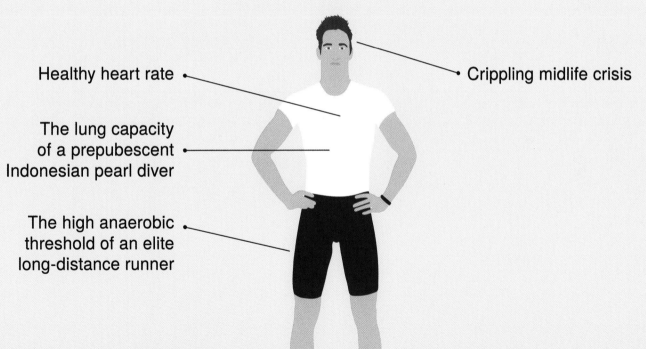

Healthy heart rate

The lung capacity
of a prepubescent
Indonesian pearl diver

The high anaerobic
threshold of an elite
long-distance runner

Crippling midlife crisis

MOST EFFICIENT WAY TO TREAT SEASONAL AFFECTIVE DISORDER

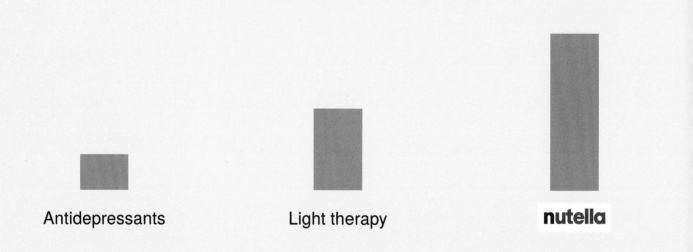

Antidepressants   Light therapy   nutella

NECESSITIES FOR PARENTS AND BABIES

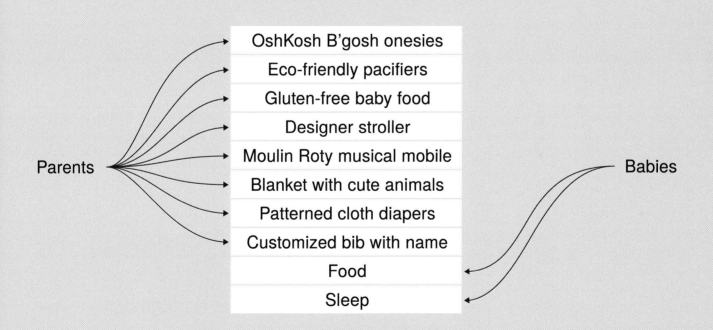

OshKosh B'gosh onesies
Eco-friendly pacifiers
Gluten-free baby food
Designer stroller
Moulin Roty musical mobile
Blanket with cute animals
Patterned cloth diapers
Customized bib with name
Food
Sleep

Parents

Babies

YOUR AMBITIONS

Before entering the job market

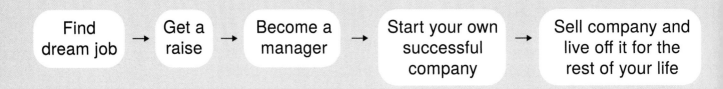

When you have a job

Keep your head down ——————————→ Retirement

WHAT YOU TELL YOUR BOSS

I've got the flu.

I've been hit with a severe case of the flu.

Someone gave me the flu.

I'm in bed with the flu.

I'm quarantined with the flu.

I'm inflicted with the flu.

The flu's got me bad.

I'm down with the flu.

WHAT YOU MEAN

I have a cold.

I'm hungover.

I'm stoned and taking the day off.

I'm super bloated from too many Doritos.

I binged on *Game of Thrones* all night.

I'm focusing on Tinder today.

I've got chlamydia.

I really need a week of vacation.

ILLNESSES

Illnesses that make us panic

SARS
Bird flu
Pig flu
Ebola
Zika virus
Runny nose

Illnesses we get

INTERVIEW STRATEGY FOR POLITICIANS

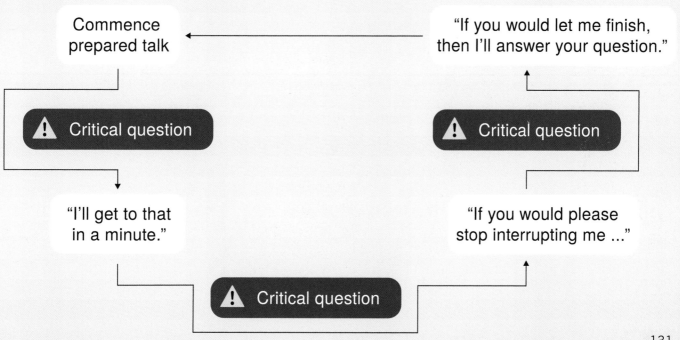

WHAT DETERMINES WHETHER YOU DANCE AT A PARTY

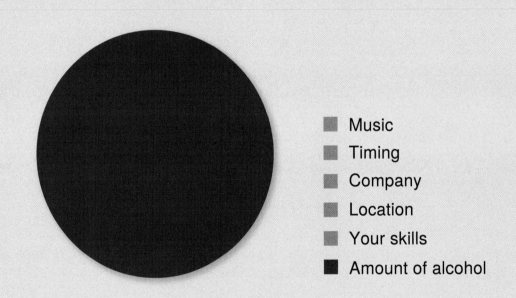

- Music
- Timing
- Company
- Location
- Your skills
- Amount of alcohol

ABOUT THE AUTHORS

Truth Facts is the brainchild of writer Mikael Wulff and visual artist Anders Morgenthaler. In addition to *Truth Facts*, they are the creative force behind the *WUMO* comic, which is printed in more than 300 newspapers in the United States. They run New Creations, a company developing and producing TV shows, movies, comic strips, online content, and books. They live in Copenhagen, Denmark.